PATRIOTIC SYMBOLS

Washington Monument

Nancy Harris

Heinemann Library
Chicago, Illinois

HEINEMANN-RAINTREE

TO ORDER:

☎ Phone Customer Service **888-454-2279**

💻 Visit **www.heinemannraintree.com** to browse our catalog and order online.

Editorial: Rebecca Rissman
Design: Kimberly R. Miracle
Photo Research: Tracy Cummins and Heather Mauldin
Production: Duncan Gilbert

Originated by Dot Gradations
Printed and bound in China by South China Printing Co. Ltd.
The paper used to print this book comes from sustainable resources.

ISBN-13: 978-1-4329-0967-3 (hc)
ISBN-10: 1-4329-0967-3 (hc)
ISBN-13: 978-1-4329-0974-1 (pb)
ISBN-10: 1-4329-0974-6 (pb)

12 11 10 09 08
10 9 8 7 6 5 4 3 2 1

Cataloging-in-Publication data avaiable at Library of Congress:loc.gov

Acknowledgments

The author and publisher are grateful to the following for permission to reproduce copyright material: ©Age Fotostock **p. 5** bottom left (Maurizio Borsari); ©Alamy **pp. 19, 23b** (Glow Images); ©AP Photo **p. 18** (U.S. Park Police, Charles Pereira); ©Corbis **pp. 10** (PoodlesRock), **15** (William Manning/www.williammanning.com), **17** (The Corcoran Gallery of Art); ©Library of Congress Prints and Photographs Division **p. 9**; ©North Wind **p. 20** (North Wind Picture Archives); ©Reuters **pp. 8, 23c** (Mike Segar); ©Shutterstock **pp. 4** (ExaMedia Photography), **5** bottom right (Raymond Kasprzak), **5** top left (Stephen Finn), **5** top right (Arvind Balaraman), **6** (Stephen Finn); ©The Granger Collection, New York **pp. 12, 14, 16, 23a.**

Cover image used with permission of ©SuperStock (Digital Vision Ltd.). Back cover image used with permission of ©Shutterstock (ExaMedia Photography).

The publishers would like to thank Nancy Harris for her assistance in the preparation of this book.

Every effort has been made to contact copyright holders of any material reproduced in this book. Any omissions will be rectified in subsequent printings if notice is given to the publisher.

Disclaimer

All the Internet addresses (URLs) given in this book were valid at the time of going to press. However, due to the dynamic nature of the Internet, some addresses may have changed, or sites may have changed or ceased to exist since publication. While the author and publisher regret any inconvenience this may cause readers, no responsibility for any such changes can be accepted by either the author or the publisher.

Contents

What Is a Symbol? 4

The Washington Monument 6

Founding Father 10

Democracy 14

The First President 16

The Monument 18

What It Tells You 20

Washington Monument Facts 22

Picture Glossary 23

Index 24

What Is a Symbol?

The Washington Monument is a symbol. A symbol is a type of sign.

A symbol shows you something.

The Washington Monument

The Washington Monument is a special symbol.

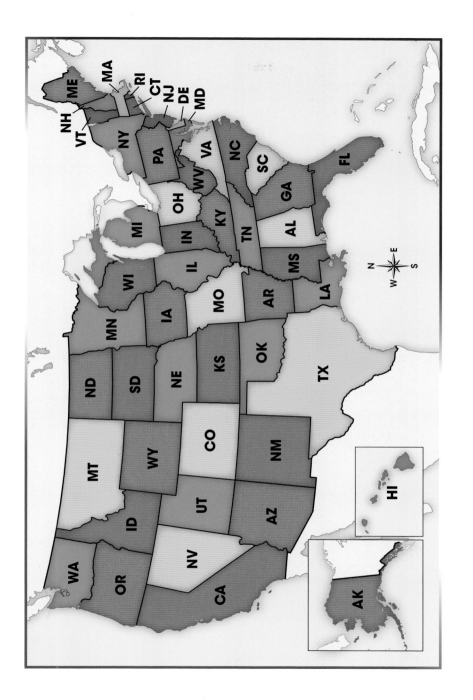

It is a symbol of the United States of America.
The United States of America is a country.

The Washington Monument is a patriotic symbol.

George Washington

It shows the beliefs of the country. It shows how George Washington is remembered as a great leader.

Founding Father

Washington is known as "the father of his country." He fought to make the United States a new country.

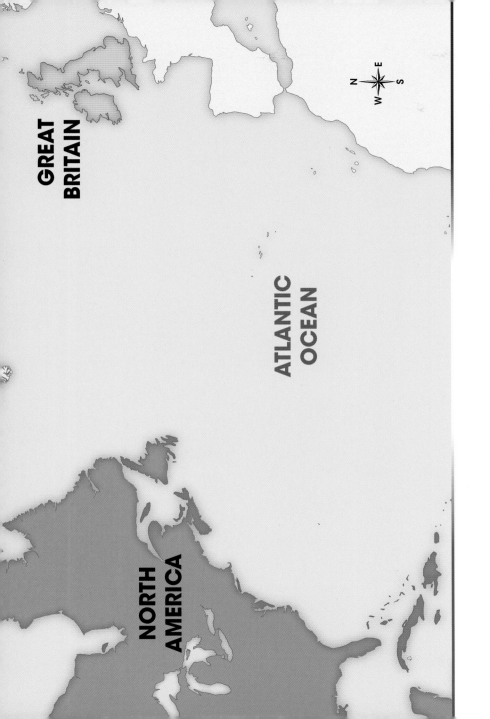

GREAT
BRITAIN

ATLANTIC
OCEAN

NORTH
AMERICA

Washington fought in a war against Great Britain.

Washington led the people to win the war.
The people created a new country.

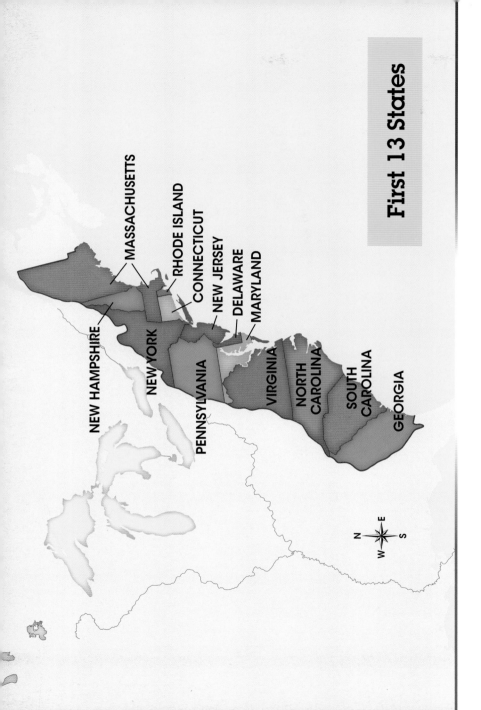

First 13 States

The monument is a symbol of how he helped to make a new country.

Democracy

Washington helped decide how the new country would be run. He helped create a democracy.

A democracy is made up of leaders who are chosen to run the country. The monument is a symbol of democracy.

The First President

Washington was the first president of the United States.

He was the first chosen leader of the new country. The monument is a symbol of how he led the country.

The Monument

The Washington Monument has four sides.
It is a very tall building.

The Washington Monument is in Washington,D.C.

What It Tells You

The Washington Monument honors George Washington for being a great leader.

It reminds us of how he helped build the United States of America.

Washington Monument Facts

★ There are 50 flags flying around the monument.

★ The flags are a symbol of the 50 states in the United States.

Glossary

democracy
the leadership of a country that is run by its people

patriotic
believing in your country

Washington, D.C.
the capital of the United States

Index

country 7, 9, 10, 11, 12, 13, 14, 15, 17

democracy 14, 15

Great Britain 11

monument 4, 6, 8, 13, 15, 17, 18, 20, 22

president 16

symbol 4, 5, 6, 7, 8, 13, 15, 17, 22

United States 7, 10, 16, 19, 21, 22

Washington 4, 6, 8, 9, 10, 11, 12, 14, 16, 18, 19, 20, 22

Note to Parents and Teachers

The study of patriotic symbols introduces young readers to our country's government and history. Books in this series begin by defining a symbol before focusing on the history and significance of a specific patriotic symbol. Use the facts section on page 22 to introduce readers to these non-fiction features.

The text has been carefully chosen with the advice of a literacy expert to enable beginning readers success while reading independently or with moderate support. An expert in the field of early childhood social studies curriculum was consulted to provide interesting and appropriate content.

You can support children's nonfiction literacy skills by helping students use the table of contents, headings, picture glossary, and index.